Read & Respond

SECTION 1

Rosie's Walk

Teachers' notes 3

SECTION 2

Guided reading

Teachers' notes 4

SECTION 3

Shared reading

Teachers' notes 7
Photocopiable extracts 8

SECTION 4

Plot, character and setting

Activity notes 11
Photocopiable activities 15

SECTION 5

Talk about it

Activity notes 19
Photocopiable activities 22

SECTION 6

Get writing

Activity notes 25
Photocopiable activities 28

SECTION 7

Assessment

Teachers' notes and activity 31
Photocopiable activity 32

Author: Sara Stanley

Development Editor: Marion Archer

Editor: Simret Brar

Assistant Editor: Tracy Kewley

Series Designer: Anna Oliwa

Designer: Anna Oliwa

Illustrations: Simon Walmesley

Designed using Adobe InDesign

Published by Scholastic Ltd,
Book End, Range Road, Witney,
Oxfordshire OX29 0YD
www.scholastic.co.uk

Printed by Bell & Bain
1 2 3 4 5 6 7 8 9   1 2 3 4 5 6 7 8 9 0

British Library Cataloguing-in-Publication Data
A catalogue record for this book is available from
the British Library.
ISBN 978-1407-12625-8

Acknowledgements

The publishers gratefully acknowledge permission to reproduce the following copyright material: **The Random House Group Ltd** for the use of extracts, illustrations and front cover from *Rosie's Walk* by Pat Hutchins. Text and illustrations © 1968, renewed 1996, Pat Hutchins (1968, The Bodley Head). Every effort has been made to trace copyright holders for the works reproduced in this book, and the publishers apologise for any inadvertent omissions.

Rosie's Walk

About the book

Rosie's Walk is a classic story; it tells two parallel stories from the perspectives of Rosie the hen and a fox. In just 32 words Rosie takes what she considers to be an everyday stroll around the farmyard. However, the book's pictures tell a very different story.

Rosie is completely unaware that a predatory fox is following her every move. Luckily for Rosie, the fox is foiled at every attempt and she returns from her walk blissfully unaware of the danger she was in.

Rosie is an enigma whose expression never changes, in contrast to the fox who carries a variety of disappointed and frustrated expressions, whilst other characters look on with bemusement. The format of the book involves double-page spreads, with alternating text and text-free pages. The text pages simply tell us where Rosie goes, using a range of positional prepositions. These pages are followed by a double-page spread with no text, this however, is where the story happens. Children will enjoy working out what disasters await the fox.

Rosie's Walk gives opportunities to develop and embellish descriptive language, show awareness of anticipation and prediction and the chance to fill in the gaps with discussion about the plot. Total immersion in the vivid, detailed pictures allows children to become storytellers as well as readers of the text and illustrations.

The book allows exploration of setting and plot among the natural environment. Increasingly children are becoming isolated from food production processes, and even those living in rural areas may have a limited understanding of farming. *Rosie's Walk* lets children return to nature and think about the animal food chain. The book follows the classic structure of beginning, middle and ending; but it is the clever and unique use of illustration that tells a parallel story alongside the story told by the text.

About the author

Pat Hutchins is one of seven children and was born in rural Yorkshire, England in 1942. From an early age she wanted to be an artist and an elderly couple encouraged her artistic talent by rewarding her pictures with chocolate bars. At the age of 16 Pat won a scholarship to Darlington Art School and then went on to study at Leeds College of Art, specialising in illustration.

Rosie's Walk was her first book, published in 1968. Since then she has written five novels and created more than 25 picture books. In 1974 she was awarded England's prestigious Kate Greenaway Medal for *The Wind Blew.* In the 1990s, Pat played the part of a narrowboat owner in the children's television series *Rosie and Jim.* Pat Hutchins lives with her husband in London, England.

Facts and figures

First published in 1968 by The Bodley Head.

Rosie's Walk was given the status of 'Notable Book' by the American Libraries Association (ALA).

In 2008 an animated version of this story was made by Scholastic.

Other popular children's books by Pat Hutchins include *Don't Forget the Bacon!, Titch, Clocks and More Clocks* and *The Wind Blew, Good Night, Owl.*

Guided reading

SECTION 2

Cover and title page

Display the cover and invite the children to describe what they see. Draw attention to the title. Ask the children to think about why it is coloured red and green. (The story is set during autumn.) The cover is also printed predominantly in these tones. What season does the cover remind the children of and why? Look for clues that might indicate that it is autumn.

Point out that Pat Hutchins uses lots of the same shapes in her illustrations throughout the book. Can the children describe which shapes she has used on the front cover and title page? Look closely and discuss the detailed pattern work, such as use of stripes, zigzags and spots.

Hold up the cover and ask the children if they know which character is Rosie. Ask: *What is the other animal and where is the rest of its body?* Open the cover out so that the rest of the fox's body is revealed on the back. Invite the children to offer predictions about the story content from the cover or title page. Point out the text on the back cover and read the blurb. Were they right?

Encourage the children to look carefully at Rosie and the fox. Ask: *Does Rosie look scared? Does the fox look frightening?* How would the children describe what the characters are doing?

Can the children work out where the story is set? What can they see that helps them to establish that Rosie is on a farm? Turn to the title page and point out the title and the author's name. Tell the children to look closely at the double-page spread and to tell you what is different from the book's cover pages. Where is Rosie? Where is the fox? What else can they see that was not there before?

Spread 1

Read the words on spread one together. Point out the capital letter in Rosie's name. Where has Rosie come from? Do the children know the word for a place where chickens live? (Coop.) Ask the children to use language to describe the fox. What does the fox's expression tell us? What do they think Rosie might be thinking about? What else can they see in the illustrations?

Spreads 2 and 3

Turn the page to the second spread and cover the text. Invite the children to guess what the text might say. Read the text together. Were they right? What doesn't the text tell us? Ensure the children have noticed the rake. Do they know what a rake is? (It is a gardening tool used to collect leaves and grass, or to break soil.) Can they predict what might happen next?

Turn over to spread three and encourage the children to describe what has happened and why. Point out the lack of text and ask if they think any words are needed. If so, what could they be?

Spreads 4 and 5

First, look at the left-hand page on spread four together. Tell the children to look closely at the illustration. Ask: *Who is watching the action? What might the frogs and butterfly be thinking or saying?* Read the text on the right-hand page. Notice how the text is positioned on the page; it looks as if it is going around the tree. What else on the page can the children see wrapped around something? (There is a flower winding around the tree trunk.)

Turn to spread five. Ask the children what has happened. What has the consequence been of the fox landing in the pond? Use words such as 'startled', 'alarmed' and 'shocked'. Ask the children if they can think of any adjectives to describe the expressions of all the animals, including Rosie.

Spreads 6 and 7

Read the text on spread six together. Have the children ever heard the word 'haycock' before? What other names have they heard or used to describe hay? Ask for suggestions of other words that could be used to describe a pile of something. (For example, a mountain of paper work or a mound of earth.) Which new animal makes an appearance on this spread?

Turn to the spread seven. Ask the children why the fox looks so fed up. Would the fox have fallen through a hay stack or bale nowadays? Discuss how hay is stored differently now, for example it is packed into different shapes and so on. Why do they think this has had to change over the years? (Health and safety, the need to waterproof and preserve.)

Spreads 8 and 9

Read the text and point out that the text is placed on the left-hand page for the first time. Explain to the children that they will have to look very carefully for a clue as to what might happen next to the fox. Look together at the writing on the sack. Invite the children to help decode the word, noting that it is written in capital letters. Where have the children seen words written in capitals previously? (In the book title.)

After turning to spread nine, discuss whether anybody had noticed that, on the last page, Rosie had her foot tied around the string and why the sack fell on the fox. Talk about pulleys and why there might be pulley mechanisms in a windmill. (To make lifting heavy things possible.)

Spreads 10 and 11

Cover the text and ask the children to predict which preposition will be used to describe the next part of Rosie's journey. (Through.) What preposition could be used to describe the fox's movement? (Over or under.) Read the text together and discuss what else can be seen in the illustrations. Do the children know what the yellow objects on the right are? (Beehives.) Why are the beehives placed on the far right of the page? Encourage the children to anticipate the fox's next move.

Turn to spread 11 and discuss what has happened to the fox and why he looks surprised. What do the children think will happen next?

Spreads 12 and 13

Read the text on spread 12. Spend some time talking about the action in the illustration. What verbs could describe the action of the cart? (For example, 'rolling', 'careering', 'thundering', 'dashing'.) Challenge the children to come up with some adverbs that could describe the way the cart moves. ('Furiously', 'dangerously', 'uncontrollably'.) Repeat the allocation of verbs and adverbs to the movement of the beehives. ('Tipping', 'toppling', 'wobbling', 'shakily', 'noisily'.)

Notice the creatures and which direction they are facing. Who are the bees looking at and why? Can the children suggest words to describe how the bees and the fox are feeling? (For example, 'angry', 'enraged', 'furious', 'provoked', 'revengeful'; 'panic-stricken', 'shocked', 'frightened'.)

Turn to spread 13. Invite the children to create sentences that describe what is happening in the picture.

Final page

Read the final sentence together. Point out the full stop and ask the children what they think it indicates. Encourage discussion about whether Rosie knew that there was a fox following her. How might she have known? Do the children think she would have heard the noises? Ask the class to recreate some of the noises Rosie might have heard. Was Rosie thinking about something else? What do the children think chickens think about? Encourage them to consider if animals can think in the same way as humans.

Review

Read through the book together again. This time concentrate solely on the words. Ask the children to guess how many words are in the book. Count the words together, noting that there are only 32.

Copy the words from the book onto the board so that the children can see the text in full. What do they notice about the sentence construction? How many full stops are in the text? Explain that the prepositions are also connective words and that they serve to continue the long sentence. Challenge the children to speak the longest sentence they can think of. Which words do they have to use to keep a sentence going on?

Ask the children if they think it is possible to read pictures. Inform the children that reading pictures is an important stage of reading. Invite the children to think about the skill of prediction and explain that they used this skill while sharing the book. Ask them what they think prediction is and why is it important when learning to read. Do they think the book could still be read without any words at all? Would it be a better book if it had no words? What if it had more? Do we need written words in books or can we just tell stories from the pictures?

Shared reading

SECTION 3

Extract 1

- Look at an enlarged copy of Extract 1 together with the class and read the text.
- Draw a chicken coop on a large piece of paper or on the board. Invite the children to help draw a visual map of the buildings and objects that they can see, leaving enough space for additional drawings at a later stage.
- Encourage the children to help construct labels for their first drawings, such as 'yard', 'Rosie', 'fox' and 'coop'.
- Return to the text and ask the children to highlight any words that they used as labels in the pictures. (Explain that these are nouns.)
- Ask the children to find a word in the text that suggests movement (*went*). Highlight *went* in a different colour from the one used for nouns and explain that it is a verb.
- Write the following words on the board: 'crouch', 'pant', 'strut' and 'stare'. Invite the children to read the words and discuss where they might be applied to the illustration.
- Read the extract text aloud again and ask the children to listen carefully for words that have the same sound in them. (The words *hen* and *went* both contain the 'en' sound.) Encourage the children to repeat each of these words after you.

Extract 2

- First look together at the illustration used on Extract 2 without reading the text. Ask: *What does the picture show?* Look at the characters and write three labels on the board: 'disinterested', 'curious' and 'hungry'. Help the children to break down and decode the words using phonological awareness. Challenge the children to allocate the labels to the characters that they think best fit each description. Explain that these words are adjectives and make nouns more interesting.
- Now read the extract text together and ask the children to add any new objects, buildings and new characters to the map they drew when working on Extract 1.
- Discuss where the objects and buildings should be placed on the map using positional language such as: 'near to', 'far from', 'above', 'below', 'left', 'right', 'next to' and so on.
- Talk together about the positional language used in this block of text (*over, past*).
- Look at the extract text and ask the children to identify any digraphs in the text ('er', 'th', 'ay' and 'ck'). Circle these as they are identified.
- Work together to label the new illustrations on their map emphasising the digraphs as they are written.

Extract 3

- Read Extract 3 together and ask the children what they notice at the end of the text (a full stop). Can the children remember any other forms of punctuation in the story?
- Explain to the class that when we read *Rosie's Walk* we are taking natural breathing breaks as we turn pages and look at illustrations. Read the whole text, encouraging the children to add commas to the text where they feel a breath may be necessary.
- Underline the words *beehives* and *time.* Can the children identify the common digraph? (The split vowel 'i–e'.) Allow the children to demonstrate how the vowel is split and by which consonants ('v' and 'm').
- Speaking clearly, sound out the following digraphs 'er', 'ee', 'or'. Challenge the children to identify the words that these sounds occur in (*under, beehives, for, dinner*); circle them on the extract. For an added challenge speak the words in a different order from their presentation in text.

Extract 1

Rosie the hen went for a walk
across the yard

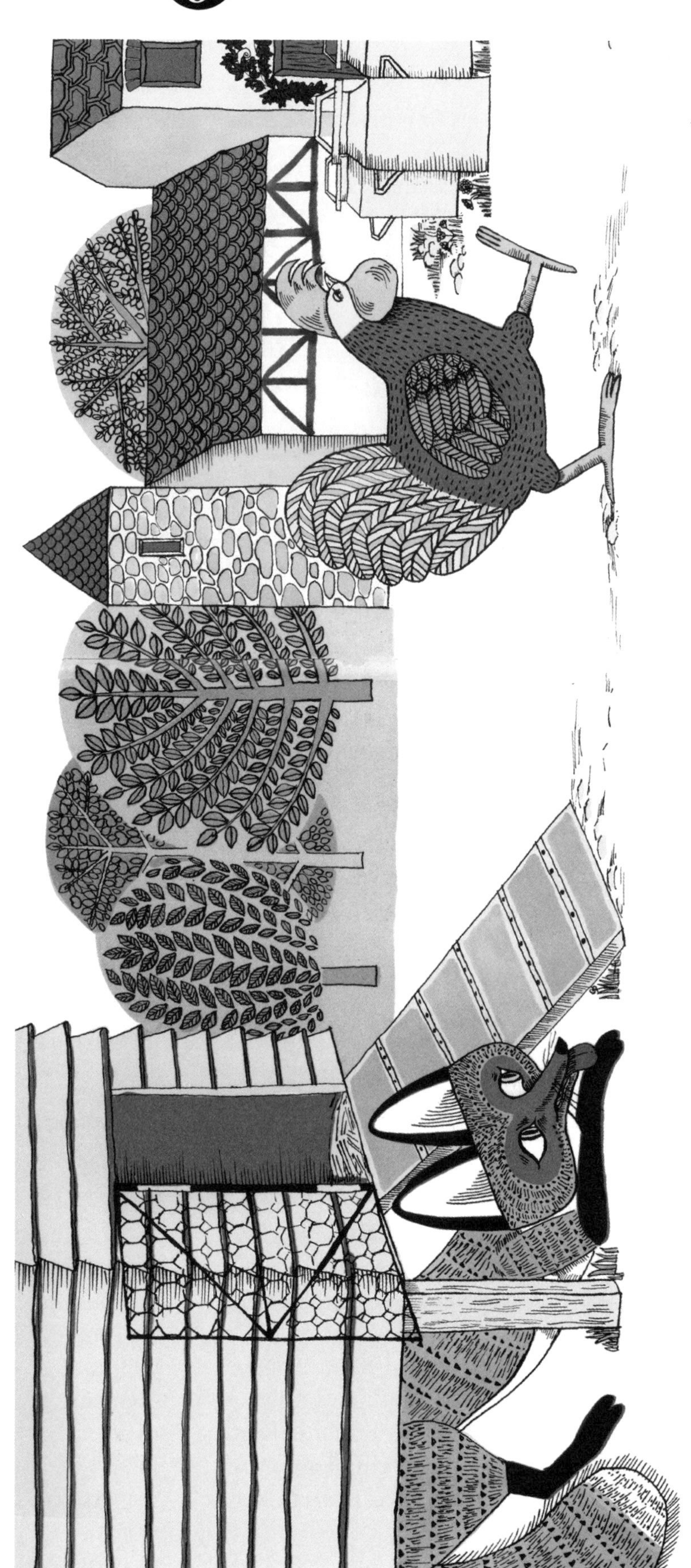

Extract 2

over the haycock
past the mill

Extract 3

under the beehives
and
got back
in time
for dinner.

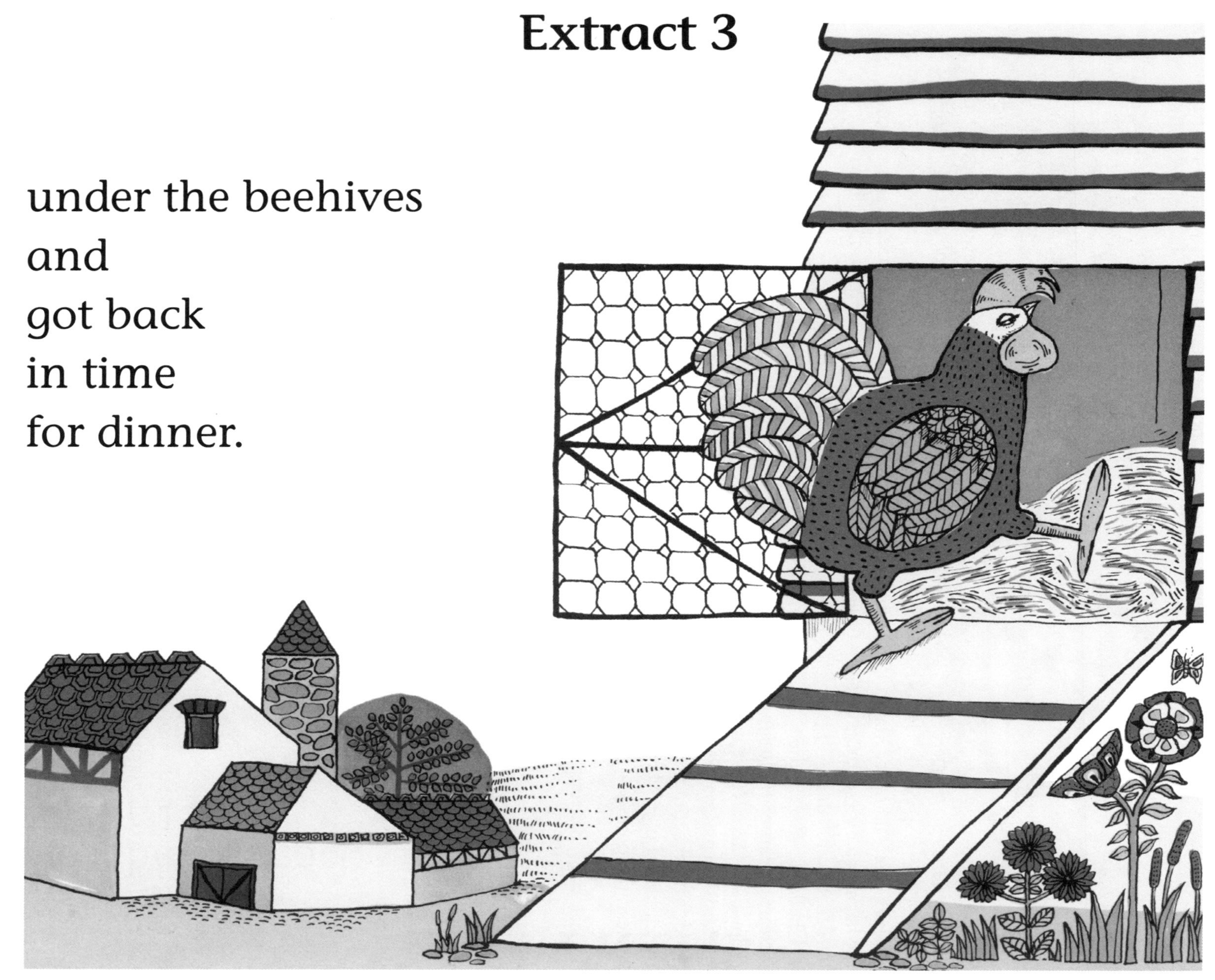

Obstacle course

Objective: To retell stories, ordering events using story language.
What you need: Copies of *Rosie's Walk*, a selection of objects to create an obstacle course (pillows/cushions, a blanket, a table and chairs/stools, a large space) and positional language labels ('over', 'under', 'through', 'around', 'past').
Cross-curricular links: PE, geography.

What to do

- Read *Rosie's Walk* together and ask the children whether the story would have been different if Rosie the hen had travelled past the landmarks of the farm on a different route. Would the fox still have met misfortune?
- Challenge the children to work together to recreate the farmyard. Invite the children to select props and materials to represent the main areas of the farm where Rosie will take her walk, such as a pond, haystack, mill, fence and beehives. Ensure the children know what each area represents.
- Read the positional language labels and place them on the floor. Ask volunteers to each choose a label and place it next to the correct landmark of the recreated farmyard.
- Encourage the children to join in with retelling the story from memory, starting with *Rosie the hen went for a walk...*
- Tell the group to follow a leader around the obstacle course, replacing the original text with the new positional language to indicate whether they would move 'over', 'under', 'through', 'around' or 'past' each obstacle.
- Rearrange the labels and repeat the exercise. Add interest by introducing verbs such as 'hop', 'jump', 'tiptoe' 'creep' and 'stamp'.

Differentiation
For older/more confident learners: Encourage the children to write their own labels and lead the processions around the obstacle course.
For younger/less confident learners: Allow the children to focus on two or three of the landmarks and labels.

Around the playground

Objective: To explore familiar themes and characters through improvisation and role play.
What you need: Copies of *Rosie's Walk*, access to an open space such as the playground, materials to make dressing-up props for feather headbands and fox's tails (for example, strips of card and feathers, orange material strips).
Cross-curricular links: Drama, PE, geography.

What to do

- Share the story again and tell the class that they are going to recreate the story outside. Encourage the children to talk together about how they can do this in the outside space available to them. What props and equipment do they already have outside and what additional items will they need?
- Collect together materials and costumes and allow the children to work in pairs, negotiating who will be the fox and who will be Rosie.
- Ask the children to re-enact parts of the story and encourage them to create new scenarios. Remind them to use the words 'across', 'over', 'through', 'around', 'under' and 'past' as they create their own versions of the story.
- Encourage the children to use additional dialogue. Ask: *What the fox might say as he follows Rosie? What might he say when things go wrong?*
- They could also use sound effects such as, splash, boing, buzz and whoosh to add drama.

Differentiation
For older/more confident learners: Invite the children to work together to script their versions of Rosie's recreated walk.
For younger/less confident learners: Allow the children to participate in small group work and use copies of the book as reference.

Hide and seek

Objective: To listen to and follow instructions accurately, asking for help and clarification if necessary.
What you need: Six shoe boxes or containers, six picture cards (depicting a yard, a pond, a windmill, a haystack, a fence and some beehives), a toy chicken and an orange scarf.
Cross-curricular link: Geography.

What to do

- After sharing the story with the class explain that you are all going to play hide and seek.
- Arrange the children into a large circle and set up the six boxes in the middle. Label each box using the picture cards.
- Ask for a volunteer to play the role of the fox and ask them to tie the orange scarf around their waist and close their eyes tight.
- While the fox has its eyes closed ask another child to hide the chicken inside or under one of the labelled boxes. (Do not place it in the box labelled 'yard' as this will be the starting point for each hunt.) When this is done the fox may open their eyes and start the hunt from the box labelled 'yard'.
- As the fox moves from one box to the next they must state whether they are going 'around', 'past', 'through', 'over' or 'under' the landmarks without actually touching them. The rest of the group may help by giving clues such as 'warm', 'warmer', 'hot', 'hotter', 'cold' or 'colder'.
- When the fox has travelled past every box, they must then decide where the chicken is hiding and they are given only one chance to reveal the hen.
- Repeat the task as often as time allows. For added variety, move the boxes around.

Differentiation
For older/more confident learners: Challenge the children to find additional descriptive temperature words to use as clues. As the fox they should describe their journey using full sentences.
For younger/less confident learners: Allow the children to focus on three of the landmark boxes.

Fox's story

Objective: To tell real and imagined stories using the conventions of familiar story language.
What you need: Copies of *Rosie's Walk*, a puppet or toy to represent the fox and a hot-seat chair.
Cross-curricular link: Drama.

What to do

- Read through the story with the class and ask the children to explain what the fox is doing on each spread.
- Explain to the children that you are going to use a drama technique called 'teacher in role'. Sit in the hot-seat chair with the toy fox. Say that you are going to tell the fox's story and that they may ask you questions about events from the book. Encourage them to ask about how the fox felt and possible reasons for his actions.
- Suggest alternative viewpoints such as, *I was trying to catch Rosie to tell her she had dropped her purse or to invite her to a party* and so on.
- After modelling this activity ask for volunteers to take over the role of the fox whilst you scaffold the other children in their questioning skills.
- Try to ensure that as many children as possible take the role of the fox.

Differentiation
For older/more confident learners: Ask the children to prepare and rehearse a list of possible reasons for the fox's actions. Encourage them to record hot-seat interviews as written stories.
For younger/less confident learners: Provide sample questions for the children to prepare responses to, such as: *What did it feel like when the bees were chasing you? Why didn't Rosie know you were behind her?*

Board game

Objective: To explore familiar themes and characters through play.
What you need: For each group of four – an enlarged copy of photocopiable page 15; a dice; two counters marked with 'F' for 'fox' – one red, one green; two counters marked 'H' for 'hen' – one red, one green; coloured pens/pencils and scissors.
Cross-curricular link: Numeracy.

What to do

- Put the children into groups of four and give each group photocopiable page 15 'Board game', a dice and sets of fox and hen counters.
- Tell the children to place the character counters on their starting point; the red hen in the red coop, the green hen in the green coop, and the foxes by their appropriately coloured barn.
- The children should take it in turns to roll the dice and move around the board counting carefully. Hens should take their turns first, so that the foxes are 'chasing'.
- They should read out and follow the instructions shown on each square that they land on.
- For foxes, the aim of the game is to catch a hen by landing on the same square before the hen makes it back to the chicken coop in time for tea. Hens must try to get back to their coops before the foxes catch them and must get the exact number to land on the square leading back to their coop.

Differentiation
For older/more confident learners: Challenge the children to create their own board games based on *Rosie's Walk.*
For younger/less confident learners: Ensure an adult or confident reader is at hand to help the children with reading out the board game instructions.

Find the fox

Objective: To experiment with and build new stores of words to communicate in different contexts.
What you need: An enlarged copy of photocopiable page 16, five pictures of foxes to use in the game, a pen, sticky tack.
Cross-curricular links: Numeracy, geography.

What to do

- Display an enlarged version of photocopiable page 16 'Find the fox' and display it to the class.
- Ask the children to help you complete the grid by filling in letters A to F down the left-hand column and numbers 1 to 6 along the top row.
- Discuss what this grid might be used for. (It is a way of telling people where to look on a map.) Have the children seen grids used in other contexts, such as treasure maps?
- Explain to the group that you will be using grid coordinates to locate the fox who is hiding.
- First practise giving coordinates by inviting them to say the correct coordinates for the other features on the grid, such as the pond (C3).
- On the back of one fox picture secretly write down a chosen coordinate, for example C4, and keep this hidden from view. Challenge the children to identify the correct square by the coordinate. Ensure the children present a coordinate in the letter/number format and encourage them to identify it on the board.
- When a child guesses correctly they may stick the fox on that square.
- Repeat the activity as necessary.

Differentiation
For older/more confident learners: Invite the children to design their own picture grid maps and to play this game independently in small groups.
For younger/less confident learners: Help the children understand coordinates by picking out certain landmarks and writing their coordinates on the board for reference (such as, chicken coop C6 and barn E4).

Predator and prey

Objective: To explain their views to others in a small group and decide how to report the group's views to the class.
What you need: Photocopiable page 17, scissors, pencils and paper.
Cross-curricular link: Science.

What to do

- Read *Rosie's Walk* and ask the children if they know what the words 'predator' and 'prey' mean. Once they have established the meanings, ask: *Who is the predator and who the prey in this story?*
- Put the children into pairs and give each pair photocopiable page 17 'Predator and prey'. Ask them to read the labels and cut out the picture cards organising them into two groups: 'Predators' and 'Prey'.
- Explain that some of the pictures on the sheet may fall into both categories (such as man). Also reassure the children that you are not looking for right or wrong answers but that you are interested in their ideas of why they think a particular animal is a predator or prey.
- Invite the pairs to share their thoughts. Make a list of the animals chosen for each heading.
- Ask the pairs to continue to work together, this time matching which prey is most appealing to which predator.
- Bring the class together and ask: *Could any cards appear under both headings? If so, why?*

Differentiation
For older/more confident learners: Encourage the children to add more predators and prey to the list.
For younger/less confident learners: Provide the children with access to non-fiction animal books to help them categorise the animals. Provide support to discuss their ideas before returning to the main group.

Mixed-up walk

Objective: To retell stories, ordering events using story language.
What you need: Copies of *Rosie's Walk*, one enlarged copy and individual copies of photocopiable page 18, scissors, glue, paper and pens.

What to do

- Look together through *Rosie's Walk*, making sure the children are familiar with the plot.
- Now look together at the enlarged copy of photocopiable page 18, which lists the positional language used in the story. As a class complete the lines of text. Do the children realise that the events are not in the correct order?
- Give each child photocopiable page 18. Tell them to complete the lines of text, cut them out and then rearrange them in the correct order.
- Ask: *Which words are missing from the sheet?* (The beginning and the end.) Think about whether the story makes sense without these extra lines. Ask: *How does the beginning set up the story?* (It tells us who the characters are and where the story takes place.) *Does the last line of text in the book tell us how the story ends?* (It only tells us that Rosie gets home safely; it does not tell us what happened to the fox.)
- Invite the children to consider the story without the illustrations. Ask: *Do the words provide enough information?* Highlight how important it is that the reader reads both the text and illustration.
- Let the children illustrate the story themselves, using the text strips.

Differentiation
For older/more confident learners: Challenge the children to make their own books with the text strips and to add text written from the fox's point of view.
For younger/less confident learners: Help the children decode sentences by illustrating key words from the text on the board first. Allow them access to the book when ordering the events.

Board game

- Choose a counter and play the game. If you are a hen, you must try to get home safely. If you are a fox, you need to catch a hen before they get back to their coop.

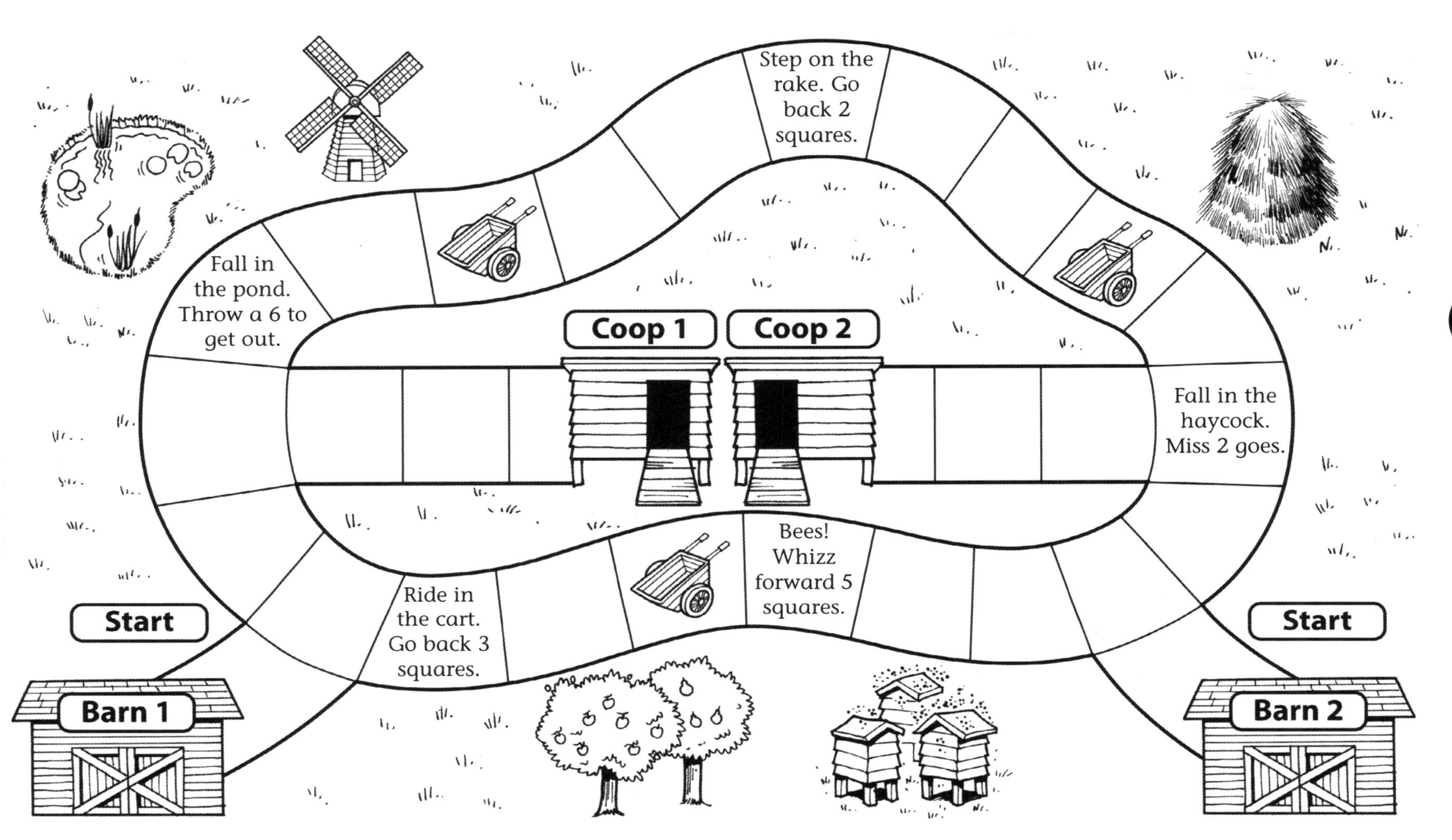

Find the fox

- Plot coordinates on the grid below to find the hidden fox.

Predator and prey

- Cut out the animals and write down the two headings 'predator' and 'prey'. Then arrange the animals under these two headings. You may need an additional heading titled 'both'.

Spider	Wasp
Shark	Man
Wolf	Sheep
Lion	Worm
Chicken	Monkey

Mixed-up walk

- Complete the lines of text from *Rosie's Walk*.
- Cut them out and arrange them in the correct story order.

around...

past...

under...

across...

through...

over...

SCHOLASTIC
www.scholastic.co.uk

Talk about it

SECTION 5

Sound walk

Objective: To retell stories, ordering events using story language.
What you need: Copies of *Rosie's Walk*, a selection of percussion instruments, a large space (school hall or outdoor area) and props to use as farmyard landmarks (for example, cushions, blanket, table and chairs/stools).
Cross-curricular link: Music.

What to do

- Read *Rosie's Walk* together and encourage the children to explore, through movement, the ways the fox would have moved. Ask: *How would the fox have moved to avoid detection? How might it have moved as it was chased away by the bees?* Invite them to demonstrate how Rosie might walk.
- Challenge the children to work together to recreate the noisy farmyard, placing cushions, chairs and other props around the large space.
- Ask the children to walk around this 'farmyard' space and discuss what happens to the fox at each location. Encourage them to use descriptive language and to represent noises vocally using appropriate volume and expression, such as 'crash', 'splash', 'thud', 'woosh', 'wheeeee' and 'buzz'.
- Allow the children to explore sounds using a variety of instruments. Discuss which instruments should be used to represent the sound effects of the story then allow the children to follow a leader around the 'farmyard', playing the chosen instruments.

Differentiation
For older/more confident learners: Encourage the children to add sequenced movements as they move around the farmyard.
For younger/less confident learners: Allow the children to focus on two parts of the farmyard and to simply use vocal sound effects.

Dangerous creatures

Objective: To ask and answer questions, make relevant contributions, offer suggestions and take turns.
What you need: Enlarged copy of photocopiable page 22, a skipping rope, labels saying 'most dangerous' and 'least dangerous'.
Cross-curricular links: PSHE, philosophy.

What to do

- Read *Rosie's Walk* together and explain that the fox is a 'predator'. Ask the children what they think the word 'predator' means. Explain that a predator stalks another creature with the intention of killing it.
- Display the enlarged copy of photocopiable page 22 'Dangerous creatures' and show the class the pictures of the creatures. Tell them that they will be working together to order the creatures from 'least dangerous' to 'most dangerous'.
- Ask the children to think silently for a minute about this task.
- Remind them that only one person must speak at a time.
- Spread out the skipping rope and place the labels at opposite ends. Cut out the pictures and ask for volunteers to place the picture cards along the rope, giving reasons for their thinking and justifying their positioning.
- When all the picture cards have been placed, ask: *Are there any cards that you would move elsewhere? If so, why?*

Differentiation
For older/more confident learners: Push for deeper thinking with questions, such as: *What is the most dangerous thing in the world? Is danger always bad?* Ask the children to provide reasons for their thinking so you can check for logic and consistency.
For younger/less confident learners: Allow the children to work in pairs and encourage them to focus on only three of the animals: tiger, crocodile and man.

Talk about it

SECTION 5

Follow me home

Objective: To listen to, give and follow instructions accurately, asking for clarification if necessary.
What you need: Enlarged copy of photocopiable page 23 and individual copies, pencils, clipboards or tables, a large sheet of paper and a compass.
Cross-curricular links: Numeracy, geography.

What to do

- Display the enlarged copy of photocopiable page 23 and show it to the class. Point out where Rosie must start and finish her journey.
- Explain that you would like the children to work in pairs to guide Rosie home across the grid and that her destination has to be kept secret from the fox.
- On a large sheet of paper draw a compass and add the labels 'north', 'south', 'east' and 'west'. Check that all children understand these directions.
- Hand out photocopiable page 23 and ask the children to sit in pairs facing each other, so they can't see each other's papers.
- Ask them to decide who will be the guide first.
- The speaker must give verbal directions to their partner using compass directions, for example: *Move four squares west, then two squares north.*
- The listener must follow the instructions, drawing their progress with a pencil.
- There are two routes home so ask the partners to swap roles to find a second way home.

Differentiation
For older/more confident learners: Challenge the children to make an 8 by 8 grid and place 10 obstacles in such a way to make the route challenging.
For younger/less confident learners: Allow the children time to work out and draw the route first before giving the directions to their partner.

Who am I?

Objective: To ask and answer questions, make relevant contributions, offer suggestions and take turns.
What you need: Copies of *Rosie's Walk*, one cut-out animal picture for each child taken from photocopiable page 24, sticky tape and a space large enough to move freely in (for example, school hall).

What to do

- Show the class the illustrations in *Rosie's Walk* and invite them to pick out and identify all the animals they can see.
- Explain to the class that you are all going to play a game called 'Who am I?'
- Attach an animal picture-card to the back of each child using sticky tape.
- Tell the children they must take turns to ask each other questions to discover which farmyard animal is taped to their back.
- Before they start the activity, discuss what questions they could ask to find out the required information. For example: *Am I bigger than a horse? Do I eat meat? Do I live in a stable?*
- Instruct the children to move around the space asking each other questions that require a 'yes' or 'no' answer. They must continue to ask questions until they have enough information to guess which animal they are, but they should not reveal their guess yet.
- When all the class is together invite each child to reveal which animal they think they are.
- Discuss which questions were helpful and which didn't give as much information.

Differentiation
For older/more confident learners: Challenge the children by limiting the number of questions that they can ask to a maximum of five.
For younger/less confident learners: Provide the children with a set of questions to ask to help them identify which animal they are.

Talk about it

SECTION 5

Memory walk

Objective: To listen with sustained concentration, building new stores of words in different contexts.
What you need: Copies of *Rosie's Walk*.
Cross-curricular link: PSHE.

What to do

- Read *Rosie's Walk* to the class and, as you read, show the children each illustration spread.
- Tell the children that you are going to play a memory activity. Close the book and challenge them to remember as many things as they can from the illustrations. Ask: *What other things might you see on a farm?*
- Arrange the children in a circle. Explain that they are going to go on a 'memory walk' and that the aim of the exercise is to listen carefully, concentrate and remember what has happened on the 'memory walk'.
- Start the walk with the sentence: *Rosie the hen went on a walk and on that walk she saw a…*
- The next child should repeat this sentence but add an additional item to the list, for example: *Rosie the hen went on a walk and on that walk she saw a tree… and a river…*
- Invite the children to add things that Rosie sees on her walk, building up the sentence.
- Repeat this exercise replacing a walk on the farm with a walk in another setting, such as the seaside. Ask: *Where else could Rosie go and what would she see there?*

Differentiation
For older/more confident learners: Encourage the children to use adjectives to describe objects and buildings, such as 'whirling windmill'.
For younger/less confident learners: Allow the children to work in smaller groups so that they have fewer things to remember.

Clever farmer

Objective: To take turns to speak, listen to each other's suggestions and talk about what they are going to do.
What you need: Pieces of paper and pens; toy props such as 'fox', 'hen' ,'farmer', 'cart' and 'sack of corn'.

What to do

- Tell the children that they are going to try and solve a problem that a farmer has.
- Present the class with the following dilemma and use the props to demonstrate: *The farmer has to leave the farm for the day. The chicken coop has broken, and the barn is locked so he cannot put the corn crop away safely. There is also a fox on the loose. He must go to the market. He can only take one extra thing with him on his cart. But he can take as many trips as he needs. What should he do?*
- Remind the children that the fox likes to eat hens, and that hens like to eat corn.
- Tell the children to work with a partner or in small groups to make a plan of action for the farmer. They might wish to record their ideas on paper. Prompt them with questions, such as: *If the farmer leaves the fox and the hen what will happen? Can he take the corn? If not, why not?*
- At the end of the activity, invite the children to share their ideas with the rest of the class. Encourage the children to make diplomatic suggestions if they see any flaws in the plans of other pairs. What would they do instead?

Differentiation
For older/more confident learners: Challenge the children to research similar problems or create their own version of this one using different props.
For younger/less confident learners: Provide the children with several plans of action that they must debate. Then ask them to decide which is the best option for the farmer.

Dangerous creatures

- Cut out the six creatures and, in your group, decide which order you would place them in, starting from least to most dangerous. Talk and think together about why you have made these choices.

Follow me home

- Listen carefully to your partner as they provide compass directions and guide Rosie home past the obstacles, without being caught by the fox. Can you find both safe routes?

	1	2	3	4	5	6
a	FINISH					
b						
c						
d						
e						
f						START

Who am I?

- Your teacher will assign you one farmyard animal (placing it on your back so you cannot see it). You will need to ask questions to discover which animal you are.

Get writing

SECTION 6

Honey pancakes

Objective: To convey information and ideas in simple non-narrative forms.
What you need: Copies of *Rosie's Walk*, enlarged and individual copies of photocopiable page 28 (makes 4–6 pancakes), frying pans, scales, spoons, forks, plates, aprons, oil, flour, eggs, milk and honey.
Cross-curricular link: Design and technology.

What to do

- Read *Rosie's Walk* then ask the class to consider what happens on a farm. Discuss how produce is grown and made from animal products.
- Look through the book and find examples of food stuffs, such as corn, flour, honey, apples and eggs (there is a nest of eggs in the tree). Talk about which of these products are used to make other things. (Flour is used to make bread and corn is used to make cornflakes.)
- Invite the children to think of other things that we could get from the farm and make a list.
- Explain to the children that they will be making honey pancakes using ingredients from the farm. Ask them to guess what they need.
- Put the children into groups of six. Work with each group and help them to make the pancakes using the ingredients on photocopiable page 28. (Make sure you check for any allergies.)
- Enjoy the pancakes then talk again about the process of making them. Ask: *What did you enjoy most about making the pancakes? Did you find them easy or difficult to make?*
- Give each child photocopiable page 28 and encourage them to write simple instructions of how they made the pancakes.

Differentiation
For older/more confident learners: Challenge the children to use recipe books and create further recipes using ingredients produced on a farm.
For younger/less confident learners: Prepare the children by sharing illustrated recipe books. Ask them to draw their recipe cards and provide key words on the board for the writing task.

Farmyard food

Objective: To convey information and ideas in simple non-narrative forms.
What you need: Photocopiable page 29, pencils, a selection of food items to create a display (such as, a box of cornflakes, cheese, milkshake, jam, crisps, bread, tinned ham, tin of meatballs, tin of vegetable soup) toy farm equipment.
Cross-curricular link: Science.

What to do

- Tell the children that you are going to investigate farmyard food.
- Show the class the items of food you have collected. Ask: *Where do you think these food items have come from?* Tell the children that they have all been made from things produced on a farm. Invite the children to think about whether they have come from animals or been grown.
- Explain that there are two methods of farming. 'Arable farming' is where things are grown; 'livestock farming' is where animals are used to make food products including meat.
- Distribute photocopiable page 29 'Farmyard food'. Read out a list of the following foods and ask the children to write the food items under one of the headings: 'arable' or 'livestock'. Food list: sausages, parsnips, yoghurt, maize, eggs, bacon, ham, milk, potato, sugar beet, wheat and beef.
- Let the class set up a display of food items. Encourage the children to write labels explaining where the products have come from.

Differentiation
For older/more confident learners: Challenge the children to look through ingredient lists on packaged food and identify which products may have come from farms.
For younger/less confident learners: Allow the children to cut out pictures from food magazines and provide support to help them spell simple words.

Get writing

SECTION 6

Noisy words

Objective: To spell with increasing accuracy and confidence, drawing on word recognition and knowledge of word structure, and spelling patterns.
What you need: Copies of *Rosie's Walk*, photocopiable page 30, pencils and pens.

What to do

- Look through *Rosie's Walk* together with the class taking extra time to notice the illustrations. Ask the children to comment on all the noises that might be heard on the farm. Ask: *What animals can you see? What events happen that create a noise?*
- Ask for volunteers to demonstrate as many noises as they can that might occur on the farm and encourage the rest of the class to guess the noises being made.
- Give each child photocopiable page 30 'Noisy words' and ask them to fill in the blank spaces to complete the missing words that will create a noise heard on the farm. Also encourage them to colour in the pictures.
- Bring the children back to the circle to sound out the words they have made, thinking about the word building process. Did they have to use any digraphs? Ask: *Which words were tricky?*
- If there is time, set the children the task of identifying all the sounds you typically encounter in the classroom and around the school. Invite them to create a sound dictionary in which they log all the sound words they encounter.

Differentiation
For older/more confident learners: Challenge the children to write more noisy words on the board in the plenary session.
For younger/less confident learners: Help the children to identify the missing letters by sounding out the words with them.

Photo words

Objective: To apply phonic knowledge and skills as the prime approach to reading and spelling unfamiliar words that are not completely decodable.
What you need: A selection of letters tiles (or letters cut from magazines), digital cameras, mounting paper and a large outdoor space.
Cross-curricular link: ICT.

What to do

- This activity may be best carried out by putting the children into small groups.
- Take the children outside and look for features in the environment where they can demonstrate the use of the words 'under', 'over', 'around', 'past' and 'through'.
- Hand out the letter tiles and explain that they can use the letters to create a photograph which demonstrates the movement and incorporates the object. For example, they may choose to place the letter tiles spelling 'under' going under a fence.
- Encourage the children to place the letter tiles in the correct spelling order but challenge them to make it visually interesting. (For example, the letters may be in different shapes, sizes, colour schemes or interesting positions.)
- Remember to show the children how to 'frame' their picture using the camera before they take a photograph.
- At the end of the activity, show the children how to download, print and mount their photographs. Put all of the photographs together to create a class display of 'movement words'.

Differentiation
For older/more confident learners: Ask the children to think of and photograph more examples of prepositions, such as 'behind', 'in front' and 'between'.
For younger/less confident learners: Provide prompt cards for the children to help remind them how to spell the preposition words.

Foxes and chickens

Objective: To convey information and ideas in simple non-narrative forms.
What you need: A selection of internet sites and a range of non-fiction texts and resources about foxes and chickens.

What to do

- After reading *Rosie's Walk*, ask the children to tell you what they know about foxes and chickens. Record their information on the board.
- Ask: *What else would you like to find out about foxes and chickens?* Record their questions on the board. Encourage the children to think of the different ways in which they can find the information that they need, for example, using non-fiction books and websites.
- Divide the class into two groups and challenge each group to research their allocated subject, either chickens or foxes. Give the groups enough time to carry out their research.
- Explain that you would like them to make notes about the information they find and that each group member should write some notes.
- Bring the class together to share and record the newly acquired information.
- The class could then create two fact folders about foxes and chickens. Make sure each child writes in the fact folder.

Differentiation
For older/more confident learners: Challenge the children to make little booklets about other items or animals from *Rosie's Walk*, for example, bees and goats.
For younger/less confident learners: Support the children's research skills and annotate their ideas and information. Allow them to draw pictures for the class fact folders, helping them to annotate and label their pictures.

Walk to school

Objective: To create short simple texts on paper and screen that combine words with images.
What you need: Copies of *Rosie's Walk*, paper, pencils, a large sheet of paper to record words and access to a computer.
Cross-curricular links: ICT, geography.

What to do

- Read *Rosie's Walk* and ask the children whether they think Rosie takes the same walk around the farm every day. If Rosie were to take a different route, what other landmarks might she pass?
- Do the children take the same route anywhere on a regular basis? Ask: *How do you get to school every day? Do you take the same route everyday? What other regular routes do you take? Is the route you take by car the same as the route by foot? If so, why or why not?*
- Compile a list of regular routes taken by the children and list any common landmarks that the children pass, such as supermarket, park, roundabout. Record how many children pass these landmarks.
- Ask further detailed questions, such as: *Do you have to go 'through', 'past', 'over', 'under' or 'through' anything? Do you have to turn 'left' or 'right' or go around something?* List any words that describe how they travel on the board.
- Tell the children that you would like them to write down one of their routes on paper or using a computer. Encourage them to illustrate and annotate their journey with drawings.
- Ask volunteers to read out their routes, inviting the other children to provide feedback.

Differentiation
For older/more confident learners: Encourage the children to create imaginary journeys around other settings, such as the moon, treasure island and so on.
For younger/less confident learners: Assist the children in annotating their routes and illustrations. Give them a list of useful words to refer to.

Honey pancakes

- Write instructions for making your own delicious honey pancakes.

Farmyard food

- Listen carefully to the list of food items given to you. Sort where these food items come from: field (arable) or animal (livestock).

Arable	Livestock

Noisy words

- Fill in the blanks to create lots of noisy words.

c l u __ __

s p __ a __ __

__ __ z z

c r __ __ k

f l __ t t __ __

__ __ u d

Assessment

SECTION 7

Assessment advice

Pat Hutchin's classic picture book, *Rosie's Walk*, provides a wealth of opportunities for children to explore the power of storytelling. With the book containing so few words, the children will develop skills to read text and pictures critically.

Understanding how to read multi-layered picture books enhances the reading process. It allows children to use visual cues, predict and anticipate action, and reflect on previous events. The pictures add so many more words to the text and often the children's words tell a language-rich tale of adventure and misadventure. The language of the book focuses on a simple journey using positional language as prepositions.

Rosie's Walk gives children opportunities to develop a knowledge and understanding of the world around them, especially developing awareness of the scientific and geographical curricula. It allows them to explore the environment and create new worlds. The story can be used to explain how nature provides food and help them to accept that all creatures, including man, are part of a large food chain.

The beautiful illustrations include simple repetitive patterns and these will allow children to revisit the story and discover new details. Exploring the book requires readers to be inventive and imaginative and will help them to develop artistic and creative skills. The story of Rosie is contained in the small world of her farmyard and this serves as a metaphor for the children who are setting out on their journeys through a much bigger world.

Rosie's Walk lends itself to learning through discussion, including role play, problem-solving, drama, music and movement activities, leading to a better understanding of character, setting and plot, and fruitful discussions about all of these story elements.

This assessment activity will allow children to present the whole story on one page. It will indicate the child's ability to pay attention to detail and explain and expand their drawing.

Story map

Assessment focus: To engage with books through exploring and enacting interpretations.
What you need: Copies of *Rosie's Walk*, photocopiable page 32, pencils and colouring equipment.

What to do

- Show the class the title page of *Rosie's Walk*. Ask: *What can you see?*
- Give each child photocopiable page 32 'Story map'. Point out the similarities between the photocopiable sheet and the title page spread (such as the existence of a mill, a pond, chicken coop and so on).
- Tell the children that you would like them to complete their photocopiable sheet to retell the story of *Rosie's Walk*. Encourage them to think about what additional details they will need to add, such as other creatures and animals or features of the environment.
- Look closely together at the patterns used in Pat Hutchin's wonderful illustrations. Challenge the children to include as many patterns as they can on their sheet to make it visually interesting.
- Ask the children to draw the route that Rosie and the fox took around the farmyard, guiding Rosie safely from her coop and back again. Explain that they must add as much detail to their work as possible in the form of illustrations, prepositional labels, annotations, written explanations and so on.
- Bring the class together to share examples of their work. Encourage the children to provide each other with constructive criticism.

Story map

- Now that you have read *Rosie's Walk*, recreate the story by designing a map of Rosie's journey. Add as much detail from the story as you can.